RAINFOREST
INSECTS AND
SPIDERS

Text and photography by Edward Parker

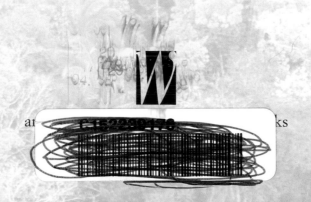

an _____ ks

© 2002 White-Thomson Publishing Ltd

Produced for Hodder Wayland by
White-Thomson Publishing Ltd
2/3 St. Andrew's Place
Lewes, East Sussex
BN7 1UP

Editor: Sarah Doughty
Design: Bernard Higton
Text consultant: Dr Paul Toyne

Published in Great Britain in 2002 by Hodder Wayland,
an imprint of Hodder Children's Books.
This paperback edition published in 2003

Produced in association with WWF–UK.
WWF–UK registered charity number 1081247.
A company limited by guarantee number4016725.
Panda device © 1986 WWF ® WWF registered
trademark owner

British Library Cataloguing in Publication Data
  Parker, Edward
  Insects and spiders. – (Rainforests)
  Rainforest animals 2. Insects 3. Spiders
  I. Title
  595.7'1734

ISBN 0 7502 3871 2

Printed in Hong Kong

Hodder Children's Books
A division of Hodder Headline Limited
338 Euston Road, London NW1 3BH

CONTENTS

① WELCOME TO THE RAINFOREST

◀ This is an orb spider from the rainforests of Cameroon in West Africa. It is in the centre of its web, waiting to catch passing prey.

▼ This pale green butterfly from the Amazon rainforest is just one species of many beautiful butterflies that live in tropical regions of the world.

INSECTS AND SPIDERS OF THE RAINFOREST

Insects and spiders are the world's most successful animals. They appeared over 400 million years ago – 200 million years before the dinosaurs roamed the Earth. Unlike the dinosaurs, insects and spiders have survived and today can be found almost everywhere on our planet. It is estimated that over 90 per cent of the world's species of insects, for example, live in the tropical rainforests.

Rainforests are found in a belt around the Equator between the tropics of Cancer and Capricorn. In tropical areas, temperatures are high and rainfall is greater than 2,000 mm each year. Rainforests are found mainly in the Amazon region of South America and in parts of Central America, Africa, South-east Asia and Australasia.

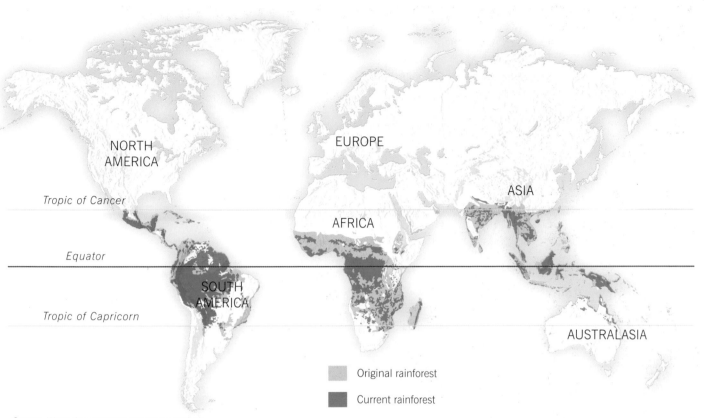

NORTH
AMERICA

Tropic of Cancer

Equator

SOUTH
AMERICA

Tropic of Capricorn

EUROPE

ASIA

AFRICA

AUSTRALASIA

Original rainforest

Current rainforest

Source: *World Conservation Monitoring Centre*

▲ *A map showing the extent of the world's tropical rainforests today, compared with their coverage 500 years ago, before large-scale deforestation began.*

▼ *This beetle with its metallic body and wings comes from the rainforests of Central America.*

THE RANGE OF INSECTS AND SPIDERS

Over millions of years, insects and spiders have adapted to the rainforests, evolving into a huge range of sizes, shapes and colours. Today, there are spiders that are so large they feed on birds, and wasps so small they could land on a pinhead. There are huge moths and butterflies, some of which have wing-spans of 300 mm – twice the length of an outstretched hand. There are beetles of different metallic shades, as if they have been created from the finest precious metals. The unique features that insects and spiders have developed have helped their survival in the rainforests.

It is impossible to know how many species of insects and spiders exist in rainforest habitats. There are only a few scientists in each rainforest country who are trained in the research techniques needed to estimate numbers over such a vast area. This book will look mainly at the insects and spiders of the Amazon, the world's largest area of continuous rainforest.

TYPES OF RAINFOREST

Insects and spiders live in all types of rainforest.
The two main types of rainforest, called lowland
forest and tropical montane forest, are found
at different heights above sea level. Lowland forest
is the most widespread type of rainforest. In its hot,
humid conditions live billions of individual insects
and spiders, from parasitic wasps
and delicate damselflies to giant tarantulas.
Tropical montane forest occurs above 900 m on
hills and mountains, where conditions are generally cooler.
The cooler temperatures of tropical montane forests means
that they do not have as many insects and spiders as in the
lowland forests.

▲ *The Amazon rainforest
provides homes for hundreds of
thousands of species of insects
and spiders.*

FEATURES OF INSECTS AND SPIDERS

Insects and spiders belong to the group of animals known as
arthropods. These include all animals that have a jointed
skeleton – an exoskeleton – on the outside of their bodies.
Insects have a combination of three pairs of legs and three
distinct body parts. These body parts are made up of the
head, the thorax (middle region) and the abdomen (lower
region). Insects have a pair of feelers, called antennae, on
their heads, and many insects also have wings.

▼ *A large Amazonian wasp
displays the key features of an
insect with a body in three
sections (abdomen, thorax and
head), six legs and antennae.*

Spiders have similar features to insects, although the head
and thorax are combined, making up a single part of
the body called the cephalothorax, and an abdomen.
Sometimes these parts are all fused together to form
a single body. A spider has a pair of feelers, called
pedipalps, on the cephalothorax. Spiders also have
powerful jaws, usually with fangs. They have a
tough, jointed external skeleton, with all muscles
and organs protected inside. However, this
exoskeleton is not as tough as that of an insect's.

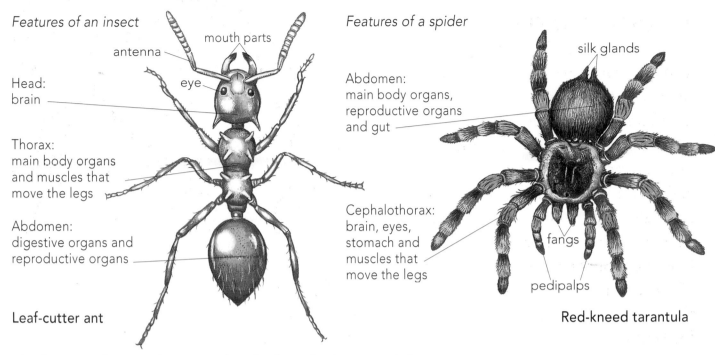

Features of an insect

antenna

mouth parts

eye

Head:
brain

Thorax:
main body organs
and muscles that
move the legs

Abdomen:
digestive organs and
reproductive organs

Leaf-cutter ant

Features of a spider

silk glands

Abdomen:
main body organs,
reproductive organs
and gut

Cephalothorax:
brain, eyes,
stomach and
muscles that
move the legs

fangs

pedipalps

Red-kneed tarantula

The features of a typical insect and spider from the Amazon rainforest.

RAINFOREST SECRETS

THE HERCULES BEETLE

The male Hercules beetle from South and Central America is thought to be the longest beetle in the world. It measures 190 mm from the top of its massive, sword-shaped horns to the tip of its abdomen. About half of this giant beetle's length is made up of its horns. One horn extends from the thorax and curves downward over the top of the head, while the other extends from the front of the head, curving forward and upward. The horns meet each other, like pincers, and are used for fighting in mating duels.

② THE DIVERSITY OF INSECTS AND SPIDERS

THE RANGE OF INSECTS

There are more species of insects on Earth than all the other types of animals combined. Estimates range from 10 to 100 million different species of insects, many of which are rainforest varieties. Around 10,000 new species of insects are discovered each year but so far only around about one million species have been described and named.

Insects can be divided into eight major groups. Each group, or order, as they are known, includes thousands of different insect species. As well as the eight main orders of insects, there are seventeen minor orders of insects. The largest of the major groups are beetles, followed by butterflies and moths.

▲ A colourful butterfly rests on the leaf of an Amazon rainforest plant.

BUTTERFLIES AND MOTHS

Butterflies and moths belong to the order of insects called Lepidoptera. Scientists believe that there could be as many as 200,000 thousand species in this order worldwide.

Fascinating Fact

Thousands of species of 'micromoths' are so small they have never been collected or named.

◄ The Atlas moth from South-east Asia is one of the largest moths in the world.

MOTH AND BUTTERFLY WINGS

One feature that sets the Lepidoptera group apart from all other insects is the thousands of tiny, overlapping scales that cover the wings and bodies of moths and butterflies. The morpho butterflies of South America can have many as 5,500 scales per square centimetre covering their wings (see above) and bodies. The scales are formed in a huge variety of patterns and colours.

Like all other insects, butterflies and moths see the world very differently from birds and mammals. Their compound eyes are receptive to ultraviolet light, which is invisible to us. The patterns on their wings are used for camouflage and for warning off predators. These patterns have to be visible to predators that see in normal daylight. At the same time, the same wings display different patterns to insects that see only bright and dark shades but no range of colours. These 'invisible' patterns are believed to be important for finding the right mate.

Butterflies and moths are some of the biggest and most beautiful of the rainforest insects. The Atlas moth of South-east Asia, for example, has a wing-span of up to 240 mm. The morpho butterflies of South America have beautiful metallic blue wings, which catch the light as they fly. There are also thousands of smaller butterflies, such as the heliconids. While the heliconids are not as large as morphos, they often have the most intricate patterns on their wings.

There are greater numbers of species of moths than of butterflies. Because most moths are active at night rather than the day, it is more difficult for scientists to observe them – so night-flying moths have not been studied as widely as daytime species.

▼ With their metallic wings, morpho butterflies are highly visible in the rainforests of South and Central America.

There are many wasps in the Amazon rainforest and they range in size from less than 2 mm to 40 mm in length. This medium-sized wasp preys mainly on small spiders.

ANTS, BEES AND WASPS

Ants, bees and wasps belong to the order called Hymenoptera. They all have distinctive narrow waists. Wasps and bees exist in a wide range of colours and sizes. There are some giant wasps, such as the psion spider-hunting wasp, which are more than 40 mm long. Others, such as the wingless wasps that pollinate figs, are less than one millimetre long.

BEETLES

Beetles belong to the order Coleoptera. So far, nearly 400,000 species of beetle have been described scientifically, but scientists are certain there are tens of thousands of beetles that have not yet been discovered. Beetles account for around one-third of all animal species on Earth, but this could increase to more than half as new species of beetles are found.

One feature that is common to all beetles is the wing covers that join in a straight line down their backs. Otherwise, they are varied in terms of their sizes, shapes and colours. Beetles have varied lifestyles, too.

Many types of beetle that belong to the scarab family have big horns. This rhino beetle uses its horns to fight other males when looking for a mate.

▲ Many insects in the rainforest are similar to species that live in temperate zones. This is a tropical montane forest ladybird.

Some beetles are predators, such as the group popularly known as 'ladybirds', which prey on small insects called aphids (such as greenfly). Others are sapsuckers or plant-eaters, while others, such as the dung beetle, are scavengers, who feed on waste material.

DRAGONFLIES AND DAMSELFLIES

Dragonflies and damselflies form the order Odonata. Dragonflies and damselflies both have long, slender bodies and large, transparent wings. They are also skilful fliers – some dragonflies can fly at nearly 60 kph. They catch other insects, mainly flies, on the wing. Dragonflies range in size from 25 mm to 130 mm in length, but we have seen from fossil records that there were once dragonflies with a wing-span of 900 mm.

RAINFOREST SECRETS

HELICOPTER DAMSELFLIES

This helicopter damselfly (see right) is part of a group that lives in the dimly lit parts of the Amazon rainforest, close to the forest floor. While dragonflies' wings are always open, damselflies are able to fold in their wings parallel to their bodies when resting. Although they are slow fliers they are agile enough to catch prey, such as flies, while on the move. The yellow eye spot visible on the transparent wings may help to confuse a predator by startling it or making it attack the wing rather than the body, giving the damselfly extra time to escape.

GRASSHOPPERS, CRICKETS, LOCUSTS AND KATYDIDS

Orthoptera is the order of insects that includes grasshoppers, crickets, locusts and katydids, which are similar to grasshoppers. There are an estimated 25,000 species of Orthoptera, and more than seven out of ten of these species live in the rainforests. These insects are all plant-eaters. The species all have delicate wings at the back, and usually have strong, straight wings at the front. They also have specialized legs that they use for making great leaps. Some species can also use their legs to make loud sounds. Most species are green or brown for camouflage, but a few species of grasshoppers are brilliant colours. Katydids have long horns and can grow to become very large insects.

CICADAS, APHIDS AND HOPPERS

About 50,000 rainforest species belong to the order Homoptera. The group includes cicadas, aphids and hoppers. The common feature of these creatures is that they

▲ An Amazonian cricket sits on a plant, probably having a rest after a meal of leaves. By remaining still and sitting parallel to a twig it hopes to avoid being seen by birds and other predators.

CICADAS

Cicadas are not just the largest members of the order, Homoptera, but the largest of all the various types of insects that suck plant juices, from beetles to aphids. Some Asian cicadas, for example, have wing-spans that reach 215 mm. However, because plant juices are often not very nutritious, cicadas can take up to 12 years to become adults.

This cicada (see right) is from the Amazon rainforest. Cicadas live high up among the rainforest trees and are often difficult to see. However, they are very easy to hear. By vibrating special membranes on their abdomen, some species can make a very loud noise. An African cicada was once recorded as making a noise similar to a passenger aeroplane taking off at an airport.

▼ *Spine bugs are a type of hopper that fold their wings up on their backs into a tent-like shape. This helps them to look like spines and camouflages them perfectly on thorny bushes.*

have mouthparts for sucking plant juices. Otherwise, they are a varied group and display a huge range of size and colours. Cicadas are the largest species. They look quite similar to locusts and can grow to over 200 mm in length. Aphids are usually less than 3 mm long and are often wingless. Hoppers are about 5–10 mm in length, with raised wing covers. Their back legs are used for leaping. Both aphids and hoppers produce honeydew, a sugary substance that is collected by some species of ants. In return for the honeydew, the ants provide some protection for the aphid or hopper.

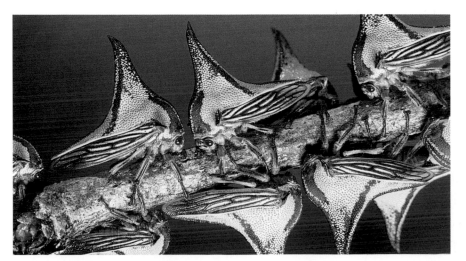

◀ The word 'bug' is often used as a general term to describe all insects. However, scientists use the term 'true bugs' for a group of insects, like this one, that fold their wings in an 'X' shape when resting.

TRUE BUGS

Another order of insects is known as Hemiptera, or true bugs. True bugs are quite similar to some species of beetles, but unlike beetles their wing covers are folded over one another when at rest. Over 20,000 species of true bugs are known to live in the rainforest, but this may be very much lower than the actual number. Many true bugs, such as the assassin bug (see page 26) and the waterboatman, have sucking beaks. Most true bugs live on plant juices, but just as many use their beaks to suck the juices out of the internal organs of other insects.

FLIES

Flies belong to the order Diptera. There are over 100,000 species of Diptera in the rainforest. Flies are amazing acrobats and are skilful at flying. Some species of horseflies can fly at speeds of up to 90 kph. There are even giant flies with wing-spans of over 70 mm and species, such as scorpion flies, which catch prey in flight. Some species of flies, including mosquitoes and tsetse flies, are parasites and carry bacteria and viruses that cause diseases.

▼ There are hundreds of thousands of species of flies, like this one, that live in the Amazon rainforest. Many of them are scavengers and eat decomposing animal and vegetable material.

PRAYING MANTIS

Praying mantis (see right) are expert predators and masters of disguise. They are generally long, thin and pale green or brown in colour. This helps them to blend in with the foliage as they wait for unsuspecting victims, such as bees or butterflies, to come along. To help their disguise they make slow rocking movements, mimicking the way foliage moves in a breeze.

When an opportunity arises to catch their prey they move with lightning speed, grabbing the victim with their powerful front legs. Their legs are covered in vicious forward-pointing spines, which they use to spear their prey.

Praying mantis have only a single ear, which is in the middle of their underside.

They cannot detect which direction a sound is coming from because this is only possible when an animal has two ears, spaced apart. When they fly, they can become easy prey for bats because they cannot detect from which direction the bat is coming.

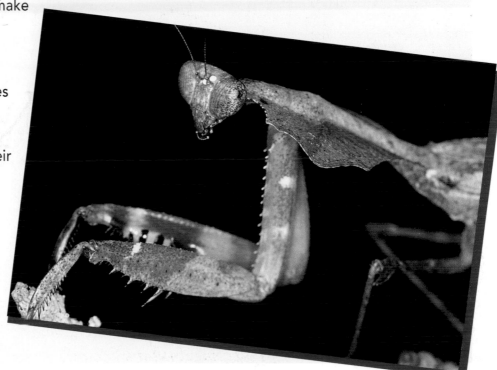

◀ Stick insects, like this one from the Amazon rainforest, often mimic leaves and twigs for camouflage.

THE MINOR ORDERS OF INSECTS

There are minor orders of insects, which include praying mantis, termites and cockroaches. Other well-known examples of insects from minor orders include stick insects, mayflies, springtails, caddis flies, earwigs and stoneflies. However, because new insects are being discovered all the time, it is likely that new orders of insects will be found. Researchers are continually discovering more about the way that insects live, and finding new ways of dividing up insects into groups.

◀ This tarantula from the Amazon rainforest is typical of mygalomorph spiders. It is very large, lives on the forest floor and catches its prey using speed and surprise rather than trapping it in a web.

THE RANGE OF SPIDERS

There are far fewer species of spiders than insects. It is thought that there are 60,000 species of spider, half of which live in the rainforests. Spiders can be divided into two general groups: the mygalomorph group, sometimes called the primitive spiders and the areneomorph group, also known as true spiders. Although all spiders can spin webs, one of the main differences between the two groups is that the primitive spiders are the rainforest wanderers, who live mainly on the forest floor, while the true spiders are better known as intricate web-builders and live at all levels of the rainforest.

MYGALOMORPH SPIDERS

Mygalomorph spiders make up only a small number of all species of spider, although they are the largest in size of all spiders in the rainforest. These include many of the large, hairy bird-eating spiders, such as the trapdoor spiders of

Fascinating Fact

The goliath bird-eating spider can grow to have a body 90 mm long and a leg span of 260 mm.

RAINFOREST SECRETS

DANGEROUS SPIDER FANGS

Mygalomorph spiders conceal their sharp, poison-injecting fangs (see right) below their head. They only reveal them when they raise themselves up on their back legs before injecting fast-acting venom into their victim, which paralyses it. Once paralysed, the rich juices are sucked from inside the prey.

The fangs of mygalomorph spiders can also be dangerous during mating. The large female may kill the male as it approaches. However, some species of fully grown male mygalomorph spiders have developed special hooks on their front legs. These are designed to hook under the female fangs and prevent her from making a fatal downward strike. Many males, however, are exhausted after mating and are attacked by the female as they retreat.

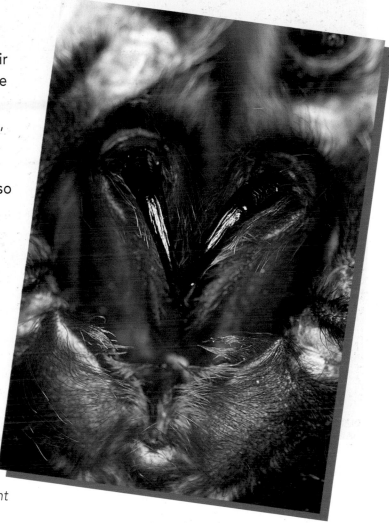

▼ *This baboon spider is a mygalomorph that lives in the rainforests of Africa. It has poor eyesight and relies on feeling vibrations to catch its prey.*

the Australian rainforest. Like other mygalomorph spiders, the trapdoor spiders hide in burrows in the ground. They set a trap with silk tripwires over the burrow and spring out of the burrow if an insect should touch one of its silk tripwires. Mygalomorph spiders have dangerous, downward-pointing fangs, which they use to strike down on their prey on a hard surface, such as on the forest floor.

ARENEOMORPH OR TRUE SPIDERS

Areneomorph or true spiders, are the classic web-builders that make up most of the estimated 30,000 species of spiders that live in the rainforests. These spiders are generally smaller than the primitive spiders and are expert silk-spinners. The silk for their web is produced in the spider's abdominal glands, which are called spinnerets.. Webs provide the spider with shelter, a lifeline, a cocoon for its young and a diving bell to provide it with air if the species hunts underwater. The web is also a means of catching prey. Areneomorph spiders build complex webs to trap insects but they are also helped by their mouthparts. The mouthparts move together in a pincer-like action, allowing the spider to catch prey on flimsy surfaces, such as its web.

▲ A Madagascan shield spider sits in the centre of its web. This type of web is spun by almost all types of areneomorph spider.

▼ The mouths of areneomorph spiders act like pincers, allowing them to bite victims on the flimsy surface of their webs.

RAINFOREST SECRETS

THE ORB WEB

There is a wide range of web shapes built by areneomorph spiders. The best known of these webs is the orb web, which spiders build in places where insects will accidentally fly into them. The Madagascan shield spider, a classic orb web-spinner, has built this web (see right).

The silk is covered in a sticky material to stop the insect from escaping quickly. As soon as a victim hits the web the spider runs out to immobilize the prey by wrapping it in silk. Some spiders inject venom before securing the victim, while others throw silk over it before wrapping it up.

Once the prey is trussed up in silk, a spider can feed on it immediately, or hold on to it for eating later.

Many of the world's most venomous spiders are areneomorphs, including the Brazilian wandering spider, which uses its fangs to inject poison into its victim.

Fascinating Fact

Some types of spider, such as the dolomedes spider, live underwater. It breathes air from a silk diving bell, which it drags underwater.

ARENEOMORPH DEFENCE

Areneomorph spiders have evolved into a vast array of shapes and colours to help their survival. For example, crab spiders are the same colour as the flower where they wait for victims. Many tropical spiders have evolved body shapes that make it difficult for predators to grab hold of them. The shield spiders of Africa and Madagascar, for example, defend themselves by using their bodies like a shield against attack.

3 THE RAINFOREST HABITAT

DIVISIONS IN THE AMAZON RAINFOREST

Lowland forest in the Amazon can be divided into the *terra firme* or 'dry land' forest and the *várzea* or 'flooded' forest. Around four-fifths of all the Amazon rainforest falls within the description of *terra firme* forest. Here the rainfall is heavy but the land rarely floods. In the *várzea*, however, the water levels of the rivers and lakes rise and fall between the dry and wet seasons. About one-fifth of the rainforest is underwater for several months every year. Another important type of lowland rainforest is mangrove forest, which is found in coastal areas.

THE LAYERS OF RAINFOREST

There are thousands of insect species living at every level of all types of rainforest, from the forest floor to the canopy. The floor of some

▲ The higher, drier parts of the Amazon rainforest are known as terra firme *forest.*

▼ The '88' butterfly lives on the river bank in the Amazon rainforest. It is recognized by the 'number 88' on its wings.

20

▲ *Euglossine bees live among the leaves of the canopy and fly between flowering trees and plants.*

areas of lowland forests, for example, is home to some of the world's largest spiders such as the goliath bird-eating spider and massive colonies of giant ants. In the middle layers of the rainforest – between the floor and the canopy – translucent-winged butterflies and mosquitoes are often seen. High in the canopy, insects such as cicadas, euglossine bees and birdwing butterflies feed on plants or collect nectar and pollen from the tops of the trees.

RAINFOREST SECRETS

THE RAINFOREST FLOOR – GIANT ANT NESTS

Some species of Amazonian ants like to make nests under large, flat areas of rainforest floor where there is little vegetation. These nests can be more than 30 m in diameter and house a colony of more than 100 million ants. They consist of a network of tunnels linking huge chambers where food is stored and where the next generation of ants is being reared. Some species of ant from Mexico create large nests from the soil close to or from under nearby roads (see right).

Other species of ant burrow underneath the roads that run through the rainforests. This is an ideal place for them to construct their nests. However, after burrowing for several years, holes start appearing in the road and the road becomes weakened. Sometimes this means that a huge chamber can collapse when a heavy vehicle is driven over it.

FLOODED FOREST

In the flooded forest, insects and spiders have adapted their lifestyles to survive the changes between the seasons. Some ants move the eggs from their low nests to higher, drier ground a few days before the water begins to rise in the wet season. Other insects migrate to areas outside of the flooded forest. Occasionally, a large mygalomorph spider can be seen swimming across small rivers as it moves towards higher ground. There are thousands of species of insects and spiders that have adapted to life in these unusual forests by migrating when the water level rises, or by spending half of their lives living in water.

▲ When the Amazon rainforest floods this beetle spends part of its life in the water. It has special back legs, which are like oars, to help it to swim.

MANGROVE FOREST

The mangrove forest is a very special type of lowland rainforest, found at the limits of the Amazon rainforest, and along nearly half of all tropical coasts. Mangrove forest has fewer species of large trees and flowering plants than other types of rainforest. Because of this there are fewer species of insects and spiders living in them. Most of the insects and spiders that inhabit mangrove forest still remain unidentified.

◀ The mangrove forests of places such as the Solomon Islands have many unique species of insects that have adapted to the salty and tidal conditions.

RAINFOREST SECRETS

CITRUS SWALLOWTAIL BUTTERFLY

The citrus swallowtail butterfly is found on the higher slopes of tropical montane forest in Madagascar and eastern Africa. These butterflies feed on the flowers of citrus trees such as oranges, lemons and limes.

Both swallowtail and birdwing butterflies (see page 45) belong to a group known as Papilionidae, but birdwing butterflies live in South-east Asia. These two types of butterflies have been separated by a huge expanse of ocean for more than 150 million years. Scientists are not sure how they are connected but they still think that these butterflies, which live on different continents, are related to each other.

▲ Monarch butterflies visit the rainforests of Mexico to breed and to complete their life cycles.

TROPICAL MONTANE FOREST

Because tropical montane forest is found at higher levels than lowland forest, this means tropical montane forests are cool and often hidden in clouds. This gives rise to their alternative name – cloud forests. Tropical montane forest is home to tens of thousands of species of insects and spiders. In the tropical montane forests of Oaxaca state in Mexico, monarch butterflies and many different types of grasshopper and cricket have adapted to the cooler conditions of these rainforests and are able to survive.

ADAPTING TO THE RAINFOREST

Over millions of years species of insects and spiders have adapted to live in all parts of the rainforest. There is huge competition between many species, which all have varied lifestyles. Insects and spiders must find enough food to eat, and find ways to survive attack. Being unique and adaptable are often the keys to survival.

Rainforest insects and spiders have such varied lifestyles that scientists have years and years more work to do before they even begin to understand how each species fits in to the ecosystem of the rainforest. The different ways that insects and spiders have developed to survive are described in this chapter.

► This heliconia flower is usually pollinated by hummingbirds attracted to its nectar. However, tiny stingless bees are small enough to enter the flower opening and feed on the sugary nectar.

▲ In rainforests around the world insects and spiders have evolved over millions of years and developed very specialized lifestyles.

Fascinating Fact

Some species of ants have ant guards for their nest. These ants can suddenly explode when the nest is under threat from a predator. By combining two chemicals, the ants erupt, spraying the predator with a dangerous mixture.

▲ *Termites are scavengers, carrying back dead and decaying material to their nests built on the forest floor.*

SCAVENGERS

In the rainforest, dead animals and decaying plant material are recycled quickly by scavengers. Scavenging insects include cockroaches, beetles and flies, all of which feed on matter from the forest floor. For example, giant cockroaches, such as the deathhead cockroach of the Amazon rainforest, scamper under the leaf litter in search of dead plant material. Flies and wasps feast on fallen fruit, and dung beetles roll dung balls back to their underground holes. Ants will pick clean a rotting body or pick up the bodies of dead insects and carry them back to their nests before they eat them.

RAINFOREST SECRETS

HISSING COCKROACHES

Hissing cockroaches (see right) are large forest floor insects. They can grow to over 80 mm in length by the time they are fully grown at seven months old. These cockroaches are called 'hissing' cockroaches because they emit a loud hissing noise by pushing air through two holes in their abdomen. They hiss when they are threatened, or when a male is attracting a female to mate.

Hissing cockroaches live on the forest floor of Madagascan rainforests. They are scavengers and feed on leaf litter and decaying plant material, such as rotten fruit.

PREDATORS

Spiders and many insects act as predators: they prey on other animals to survive. Spiders catch their prey in webs or by using a surprise attack. Mexican jumping spiders can jump 30 times their own body length to catch their prey. Giant praying mantis can grab their victims including insects, lizards and even small mammals. Wasps of all sizes often prey on spiders, and can kill quite large tarantulas by stinging them to death.

◀ *Wasps are examples of specialized rainforest insect predators. Many species of wasp hunt only spiders, which they carry back to their nest to eat.*

RAINFOREST SECRETS

THE ASSASSIN BUG

Assassin bugs are true bugs (see page 14) that live in the rainforests of South America. They are very successful predators. The different species of assassin bugs catch different prey. Some leap on fast-moving victims such as ants or beetles, while others attack slower prey such as caterpillars.

Like all true bugs, assassin bugs cannot chew but they have piercing mouthparts. When the assassin bug has caught a victim, it pierces through the hard outer skeleton with its mouthparts and injects saliva to part-digest the internal organs. The part-digested contents of the victim's body are then sucked out.

▶ The fearsome jaws of this beetle from the tropical montane forests of Mexico show it to be well equipped as a predator.

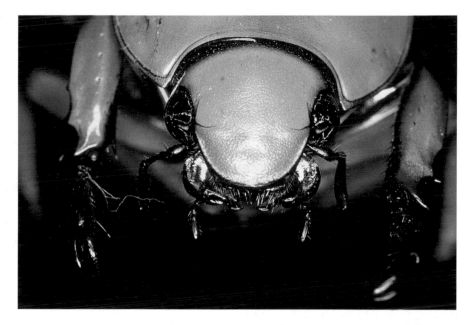

▼ A parasitic wasp has placed its cocoons on a caterpillar. When the wasp grubs hatch they will burrow into the caterpillar and devour it as their first meal.

The tarantula is then carried away to the wasp's nest to be eaten. Army ants will overcome much larger prey by sheer numbers, and powerful soldier ants can tear a victim apart.

PARASITES

Many species of rainforest insect live and feed on other plants. These parasites include many types of flies, beetles and butterflies. There are also thousands of species of parasitic wasp. Many rainforest wasps paralyse their victims, such as caterpillars, before laying eggs on or in their living bodies. The wasps feed on the host when they hatch. Some species of tropical blowflies and botflies also lay their eggs in a living host, which provides food for the young blowflies and botflies when they hatch.

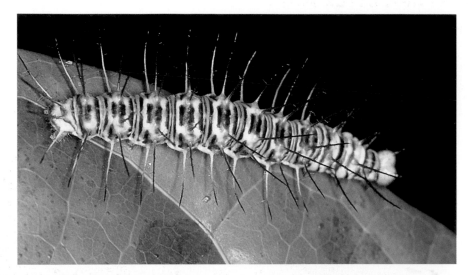

Rainforest caterpillars constantly eat plant material in order to build up enough energy reserves to metamorphose into butterflies or moths.

Fascinating Fact

Wallace's moth, from Madagascar, has a proboscis, or feeding tube, that is over 150 mm long.

Grasshoppers are vigorous plant-eaters. They can gather together in huge numbers and strip large areas of rainforest bare of vegetation.

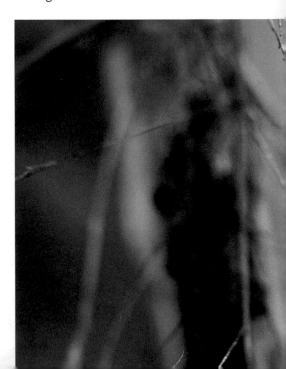

PLANT-EATERS

There are hundreds of thousands of insects that eat plants. Tropical crickets, grasshoppers and giant jungle nymphs are all plant-eaters. The caterpillars of moths and butterflies also fill themselves up with leaves and fruit before transforming into winged adults. Some caterpillars eat poisonous plants so that birds and other predators will not be able to eat them, before they change into butterflies.

While insects have evolved to eat plants, there are some plants that have evolved defences to stop insects from

LEAF-CUTTER ANTS

Leaf-cutter ants can strip a 5-m tree of all its leaves in just a few hours. All the ants carry away small fragments of leaves to their underground nests (see right). They do not eat them, but pile them up to grow fungi on. The ants feed on fungi because their stomachs are not able to digest plant material.

Leaf-cutter ants will travel up to 200 m away from their nests in order to collect plant material. Usually, guard ants protect the main lines of leaf-cutter ants. These ants are much smaller than the main lines of leaf-cutter ants and they try to stop parasitic wasps laying eggs in the heads of the worker ants.

When an ant colony gets too large, or flooding destroys the old nest, one of the queens takes a small piece of fungi with her to start a new colony.

▼ *Butterflies and moths both have special tube-like tongues that they use to reach the heart of a flower and drink the nectar.*

eating them. Some plants have poisonous spines, or produce foul-tasting or poisonous chemicals. Many insects are able to overcome plant defences. Some caterpillars, for example, cut holes in the veins of poisonous plants to stop the poison from reaching the place where they are eating.

SAPSUCKERS AND NECTAR DRINKERS

Many species of insects take advantage of other foods produced by plants, such as sap and nectar. Insects that suck plant juices, such as cicadas, pierce their mouthparts into the plant to reach the nutritious juices inside.

Nectar drinkers have long tongues so they can reach nectar, which is often hidden deep in a flower. For example, moths and butterflies are often expert nectar drinkers and have a long feeding tube, called a proboscis, which they can unroll to reach the nectar while they hover in front of it.

◀ *This ground-living Amazonian cricket blends in perfectly with the dead leaves on the forest floor.*

CAMOUFLAGE

Insects use a whole range of techniques to protect themselves. These include bites, stings, spines and poisons. One way of staying alive is not to be seen in the first place, and to do this some insects and spiders use camouflage. Camouflage is when an insect or spider remains hidden by looking like the plant it is on, or like something inedible, such as a bird dropping. Amazonian crickets, for example, merge into the dead leaves on the forest floor. Green jungle nymphs are the colour of the leaves they hide amongst and stick insects look like different parts of plants, such as twigs and stems. Some species of moths, such as the giant owlet moth, blend into the colours of tree trunks.

▼ *The giant jungle nymph is not only the same colour green as the plants it feeds on, it is also covered in fake 'prickles' to make its camouflage better.*

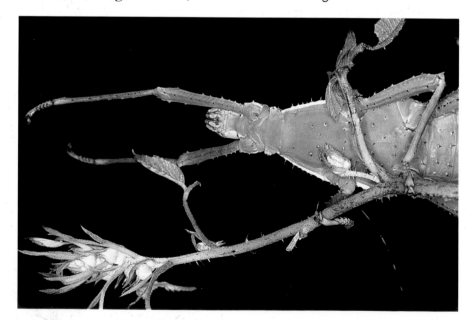

▲ Like some wasps, this bug mimics the shape of an ant, which allows it to get close to lines of ants in order to catch and eat them.

MIMICRY

Some insects and spiders can copy, or mimic, dangerous creatures as another way of protecting themselves and staying alive. Some caterpillars have eyespots and markings that make them look like snakes or other dangerous creatures. There are some strange mimics, such as a wasp that can walk backwards unnoticed to prey on ants, because its back half looks exactly like an ant. Some harmless, non-poisonous insects mimic the brightly coloured markings of poisonous or inedible insects to stay safe.

RAINFOREST SECRETS

EYESPOTS

Some insects, such as the owlet moth (see right), defend themselves by startling their predators just long enough to make an escape. To do this, they reveal markings on their wings that look like the eyes of a snake or a small cat.

The eyespots can mislead some attackers into striking at the wings, away from the moth's body, allowing the insect to escape. It is common to see moths and butterflies with damaged wings where they have been attacked.

COLOUR AND CHEMICAL DEFENCES

Poisonous insects often warn others about their defences by being brilliantly coloured. The bright colours of many species of caterpillar alert potential predators to their foul taste, or to the fact that they are covered in irritating hairs or spines. Many insects with powerful stings or bites, such as many species of wasp, warn about their defences in this way.

Many insects and spiders can make and store special chemicals. Some insects produce chemicals which make them poisonous to eat. This helps to stop predators from attacking them. Spiders produce poisonous chemicals, which are injected into their victims to immobilize them. Some species of beetles can spray an attacker with hot, dangerous chemicals or produce foul-tasting liquids or foams to keep away predators.

▲ A Peruvian fern insect displays the fact that it is poisonous by being brightly coloured.

◀ An adult and a young beetle from the tropical montane forest in Ecuador. By raising its abdomen, a beetle is threatening to spray poisonous chemicals at an attacker.

USING CHEMICALS TO MAKE LIGHT

Some insects, such as a female glow-worm and the male or female firefly (see below) can produce light to attract mates at night. They do this by combining chemicals stored in separate parts of their abdomen.

The female firefly climbs up on a plant and lights up her abdomen to attract a male. The male firefly makes pulses of light to attract a female and the female responds by flashing a message back if she is ready to mate.

Fascinating Fact

Some stingless bees make trails of scent to guide others to food.

HARMLESS CHEMICALS

Some chemicals produced by insects are not dangerous. These include the scents produced by insects to attract mates. Female moths of some rainforest species produce scents that can be detected by males over one kilometre away. Insects such as bees, moths and ants also produce chemicals that smell attractive as part of their way of communicating. An injured bee, for example, gives off a scent that encourages other bees to come and attack an aggressor that might hurt the injured bee. Female cecropia moths release an appealing scent to help males find them and another to encourage males to mate with them.

⑤ REPRODUCTION

◀ *These dragonflies are from the rainforests of Sarawak in South-east Asia. They mate on a branch or leaf close to the surface of a pond or river before laying their eggs underwater.*

MATING

Insects and spider species have many different mating rituals. Some insects, such as euglossine bees, attract mates by covering themselves in the perfume from an orchid. Crickets and grasshoppers send out sounds to attract or encourage females to mate. The shrill sound they make is called stridulating, or 'singing'. Because male spiders are much smaller than females, they tap out messages to the predatory female along a strand of a web before attempting to mate. Female glow-worms send light signals by pulsing their light-producing organs to attract a partner. Male bees vie with other bees to mate with a queen while flying. If successful, the bee has to break open its own body in order to implant the sperm and dies in the process.

GROWING UP

Usually insects lay eggs in large numbers and leave the young to fend for themselves. However, some species of

Fascinating Fact

The male praying mantis has its head bitten off by the female during the act of mating.

spiders are quite protective of their young, releasing them from the web to live on their own only after they have grown big enough to look after themselves.

Spiders and some insect species emerge from their eggs as smaller versions of their parents. Grasshoppers, for example, emerge from eggs as nymphs, which are almost identical to their parents, apart from their wings. Other insects, such as caterpillars, come out looking quite different from their parents. These insects undergo a metamorphosis to change them from a caterpillar into an adult moth or butterfly.

▲ The deathhead cockroach nymph (on the right) does not yet look like the adult (on the left) because it has to shed its skin several more times.

R A I N F O R E S T   S E C R E T S

METAMORPHOSIS

A caterpillar hatches from an egg before it changes into a butterfly or moth. Caterpillars grow by constantly eating plants. As they grow, they moult, which means they shed their skins.

When they have shed their skin for the fifth time, they change to the chrysalis stage (sometimes called the pupal stage). This is where the insect larva attaches itself to a solid object and builds a hardened shell from silk. This chrysalis (see left) is a rare golden chrysalis from Cameroon.

Over several weeks, the body structures of the caterpillar inside the chrysalis are completely rearranged before it emerges as a winged adult butterfly or moth.

THE LOSS OF INSECTS AND SPIDERS

Insect and spider species are disappearing more rapidly today than at any other time in history. Many species of insects and spiders are now becoming extinct. It is impossible to know exactly how many insect species are dying out, but the number could be greater than 10,000 species every year.

Many insect species are very sensitive to small changes in their environment, such as a change in temperature or the loss of a particular type of food. Any number of small changes can cause insect and spider species to become extinct. In the Peruvian rainforest, for example, 650 species of beetle have been found living on a single species of tree. If this species of tree was lost, the insect species would also be threatened.

The use of pesticides and the release of polluting chemicals harms insects and spiders. Also, the introduction of alien species of animals, usually brought in accidentally by humans, can also lead to the extinction of species.

▲ Burning areas of rainforest destroys the habitat of many rare species of insects and spiders.

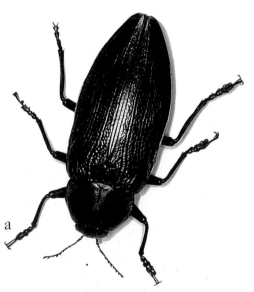

▲ Wood-boring beetles suffer in areas of rainforest that are logged because loggers often burn unwanted and rotting trees.

RAINFOREST SECRETS

AFRICAN BEES

The bees in this hive (see right) are an aggressive species of African bee. African bees are believed to have greatly reduced the numbers of native species of bee in the rainforests of South and Central America. In the late 1950s, a swarm of African bees escaped from a research project in São Paulo in Brazil. The African bees invaded the hives of many species of rainforest bee. The African queen bees were able to mature more rapidly than the South American bees so they killed all the other potential queens in the hive. This caused bees that are important pollinizers of plants to become almost extinct in the rainforests of South and Central America. The South American/African hybrid bee that exists now in South America has become more aggressive and dangerous than the African bee, but it produces more honey than the South American bee.

INSECT COLLECTORS

▼ The wild population of red-kneed tarantulas was devastated when it became fashionable in the USA and Europe to own one as a pet. Today, they are bred in captivity.

Millions of insects are collected from the rainforests every year. There is a large international market for beautiful insects and spiders from rainforests. Many thousands of local people earn part of their living by catching and selling rare spiders. This activity has caused a great loss of some of the more unusual species because collectors are prepared to pay huge sums of money for them. In this way, many of the world's rarest insect and spider species are being brought to near extinction in the wild.

The loss of their rainforest habitat is the most immediate threat to rainforest insects and spiders.

LOSS OF RAINFOREST HABITAT

There are many factors affecting the survival of rare rainforest insect species, but the most serious is the loss of their rainforest habitat. According to the statistics, 400,000 hectares of rainforest are destroyed in the Amazon every year (source: UNEP/WCMC). This destruction is to make way for roads, hydroelectric power plants, mines and the expanding rainforest towns and cities. Large areas are also being cut down so that hardwood can be sold and other areas are being used for activities such as growing soya beans, oil palms and cattle ranching.

In Asia and Africa, many rainforest countries have rapidly expanding populations and the people are struggling to find enough farmland on which to grow food. Millions of poor people try to feed their families by entering the rainforest in search of food and land. They cut down areas of rainforest in order to create land on which to grow crops. This is devastating for the rainforests.

'Greenhouse' gases are causing the world's climates to change, threatening the existence of many sensitive insect and spider species.

CHANGES IN CLIMATE

While many types of insects, such as flies and cockroaches, can easily adapt to changes in environmental conditions, there are thousands of other species that are affected by very small changes

LINKS

Mosquitoes and Malaria

There are several thousand species of mosquito (see right) living in the rainforests. These mosquitoes suck blood from many types of animals and they also prey on humans. The Anopheles mosquito carries malaria. Around 100 million people are infected with malaria every year and between one and two million people die as a result of the disease.

Mosquitoes and many other rainforest insects are unpopular with people who live in or near to the rainforest. This means that rainforest insects in general are often thought of as pests, and pesticides are used to reduce the natural populations of insects, such as mosquitoes. However, the widespread use of chemicals (see left) such as DDT (an insecticide) has had a major impact on other harmless rainforest insects as well and thousands of insect species have become extinct in the process.

in their environment. All over the world today local and global climates are changing because of human activity. Since the beginning of the twentieth century the surface of the whole planet has been getting warmer because of the release by industry of huge amounts of 'greenhouse' gases, such as carbon dioxide and methane. It is thought that the world will warm up by around 4 °C by the end of the twenty-first century. No one is certain what effect this will have on the number of species of insects and spiders in the rainforests but most scientists think that there will be a huge loss in their variety.

◀ *Scientists at the La Planada reserve in Colombia, an area of tropical montane forest, are studying insects in order to understand how best to conserve rare species.*

THE CONSERVATION OF RAINFOREST INSECTS AND SPIDERS

The conservation of rainforest insect and spider species is not considered very important by national governments, or even many environmental organizations. Many rainforest insect and spider species remain unidentified. Scientists have studied some species, but it is still difficult for them to work out exactly how important those species are and where they fit into the complicated rainforest ecosystem.

However, environmental organizations such as WWF and many local communities are working hard to protect the world's remaining rainforests. By doing this they are also helping all the plant and animal species that live in them – including insects and spiders.

▼ *Single large rainforest trees have been shown to be home to thousands of species of insects and spiders. Protecting trees helps protect these species.*

RAINFOREST SECRETS

RARE MEXICAN BUTTERFLIES

In the community of Ixtlan, in Oaxaca state in Mexico, local butterfly expert Ivan Ruiz enters the rainforest on his mountain bike, in search of rare butterflies.

In Oaxaca lives one of the world's rarest butterflies, the oaxacana species (genus Catasticta). Only five individual butterflies (see right) have ever been observed, and two of these were in the community of Ixtlan.

Fortunately, this area of tropical montane forest is owned and managed by a local Zapotec community, which is carefully managing the rainforest. While the community of Ixtlan harvest timber from parts of the rainforest, they do so in a way that is sensitive to the environment. This means that large expanses of tropical montane forest are left untouched for the benefit of wildlife.

PROTECTED AREAS

Fortunately, many of the actions that are taken to protect rare species of rainforest mammals and birds have positive effects for insect and spider species living nearby. The setting up of a jaguar reserve in Belize, for example, has not only protected the habitat of the jaguar but also the thousands of species of insect and spiders that share the rainforest with it. As the loss of rainforest insect and spider species is caused mainly by the loss of rainforest habitat, any conservation action that ensures the long-term survival of an area of rainforest is very important to maintaining the variety of rainforest insect and spider species.

To understand which butterflies or moths live in a rainforest it is necessary to catch and identify a set for reference. These moths are from the tropical montane forest in Ecuador.

RESEARCH

Much more research is needed to know how to conserve rainforest insect and spider species in the most effective ways. Without detailed information, it is difficult to know whether conservation projects are working, or even if researchers have chosen the most critical areas of rainforest in which to work. Thousands of researchers around the world are working at identifying and creating species lists for different types of rainforest. It is a very complicated task because an insect species may occur only on a single type of plant or in a very limited part of the rainforest.

EDUCATION AND AWARENESS

Education is also vitally important to conservation efforts. If people know more about how important rainforest insects and spiders are to the rainforest then conservation projects will have a greater chance of success. In many rainforest areas, local children are being taught about the ecology of the rainforest so that when they grow up they will be more sensitive to rainforest wildlife.

In many countries, such as here in Colombia, schoolchildren visit the rainforest to learn about wildlife as part of their education.

World Expert on Madagascan Ants

This Malagasy man lives close to the edge of the rainforest National Park of Andringitra. For many years he helped and guided insect experts who visited the area to work on rainforest insects. Over the years he taught himself how to carry out scientific research into the many ant species of the Malagasy rainforest.

Today, he is recognized as one of the world experts on Malagasy ant species. For example, he knows how the variety of ant species in a particular area of rainforest can give an idea of the health of the rainforest. A wide variety of ants shows that an area of rainforest has not been disturbed to any great extent. In 1997, this Malagasy expert became the first non-scientist and local person to receive the International Gold Medal for environmental work from Prince Bernhard of the Netherlands.

On an international level, people who have learned about the importance of the rainforests as homes for species of insects and spiders can take action. They can choose not to buy certain goods from the rainforest if they know that their production is destroying species of insects and spiders. People can help the rainforests by making themselves aware of good and bad farming practices in rainforest areas. They can choose to buy organic rainforest produce, for example, which does not use the pesticides that have such a serious effect on insect and spider species.

It is also necessary for governments and businesses to understand the importance of rainforests and to try and reduce the number of large projects, such as mines, which devastate the rainforest.

7 THE FUTURE

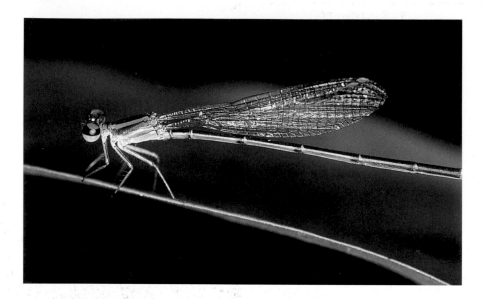

This delicate Amazonian damselfly is just one of many species of insect that have an uncertain future in the rainforests.

LOSS OF INSECT AND SPIDER DIVERSITY

The loss of insect and spider species is greater now than at any time during the 400 million years that insects and spiders have existed on Earth. We are losing rainforests faster today than at any time during their history. While some types of insects are adaptable, many species are sensitive to change and will die out even if there are only minor alterations to their environment. A large number of species could be lost by the end of the twenty-first century if action is not taken quickly.

Although cockroaches are unpopular because of their scavenging lifestyle, rare rainforest species such as this deathhead cockroach from the Peruvian Amazon deserve our protection.

CONSERVATION ACTION

Many environmental organizations are campaigning hard for governments and large companies to be less destructive of the world's remaining wilderness areas. Organizations such as WWF are campaigning for environmentally sensitive use of the rainforest so that when timber is harvested it is done in a way that causes the least damage to the rainforest.

The best way of helping insects and spiders to survive is to protect their homes. WWF has successfully petitioned many governments of countries that have tropical rainforest, to protect at least 10 per cent of their remaining rainforests.

LINKS

WWF Birdwing Project

In the rainforests of South-east Asia live a group of huge and beautiful butterflies known as birdwings. For many years their numbers have been declining, partly because people used to catch and sell these extremely rare and valuable butterflies.

WWF has teamed up with a number of communities in the Arfak Mountains of Irian Jaya in Indonesia in an effort to conserve the wild populations. A number of local projects have been set up whereby the villagers now grow the Aristolochia vine that the birdwing caterpillar (see right) feeds on. They also rear thousands of caterpillars each year, which in turn become butterflies that they can sell.

In this way, local populations of butterflies are left alone and the villagers can earn an income.

▼ The future of rainforest insects and spiders largely relies on protecting their habitat in the rainforests.

In dozens of rainforest countries, such as Thailand, Australia, Peru and Colombia, this has been a success. Many countries of the world have also signed up to the International Convention of Biological Diversity, which is aimed at protecting the variety of all life on Earth. People that choose to buy rainforest products from well-managed rainforests and from countries that have signed this agreement, could also be helping to reduce the loss of insect and spider species.

GLOSSARY

African bees.

abdomen The belly of a creature, such as an insect or spider.

alien Any organism, such as a plant or animal, that lives in an area that is not its usual habitat.

assassin bug A creature that has a curved proboscis which it uses to stab into the back of prey, like an assassin's knife.

camouflage Colours, shapes and patterns that help a creature blend in with its surroundings.

canopy The layer of trees between the forest floor and the tallest towering treetops.

colony A group of the same species that live close to each other.

conservation Protecting the quality of the environment and its resources.

diving bell A bubble of air in a silk, bell-shaped container that a spider uses to breathe under water.

ecology The study of the inter-relationship between organisms and all aspects of their environment.

ecosystem A community of different species and the environment they live in.

evolving When a species of any organism is developing by natural processes over many generations.

exoskeleton The hard outer skeleton of insects and spiders and some other creatures.

fungi A group of non-flowering plants, such as mushrooms or moulds, which live as parasites.

host An organism, usually a plant or animal, that is fed on by a parasite.

humid Usually refers to when weather conditions are warm and damp.

insecticide A substance that can be used to kill insects.

larva The stage between the egg and the pupa of insects such as caterpillars, maggots and grubs.

membrane A thin layer of tissue that some types of insects can use to make sounds.

metamorphosis To change the form of something, such as from a caterpillar to a butterfly.

migrate To move out from one region in order to settle in another.

nectar The sugary substance produced by plants and made into honey by bees.

nutritious When a food provides essential nourishment for living organisms.

parasite An organism that lives on another organism in order to gain food or shelter.

pesticide A substance that can be used to kill fungi, bacteria or insects.

pollen Fine powder produced by a tree or plant that is used in creating new trees or plants.

proboscis Any of the long mouth-parts of an insect, that can be used for feeding or piercing.

scavenger A creature that feeds on the left-overs that others leave behind.

species A group of organisms, such as insects, plants or animals that closely resemble one another.

true bugs The bugs that belong to this group are the ones that fold their wings in an 'X' shape. True bugs do not include flies or beetles, for example.

ultraviolet light (UV) Part of the light spectrum that can be seen by certain types of insects.

waterboatman An insect with feet like oars that sculls across the water rather like a rowing boat.

FURTHER INFORMATION

BOOKS TO READ
Closer Look at the Rainforest by Selina Wood (Franklin Watts, 1996)
Journey into the Rainforest by Tim Knight (Oxford University Press, 2001)
Jungle Animals by Anita Ganeri (Parragon, 2000)
The Rainforest by Karen Liptak (Biosphere Press, 1993)
Rainforest Animals (Two-Can, 1999)
Secrets of the Rainforest by Michael Chinery (Cherrytree, 2001)
The Wayland Atlas of Rainforests by Anna Lewington (Hodder Wayland, 1996)

WEBSITES
There are many websites about the rainforests. Type in key words to search for the information you need, or visit the following sites:

Passport to the Rainforest
http://www.passporttoknowledge.com/rainforest/main.html
Includes map, graphics, images and information about plants and animals.
Rainforest Action Network
http://www.ran.org/
Facts about rainforest people and animals presented in a question and answer format. Includes action that children can take to conserve the rainforests.
Rainforest Conservation Fund
http://www.conservation.org/
Provides species data for plants and animals including news, projects and articles.
Rainforest Information Centre
http://www.rainforestinfo.org.au
News, information, ecology and conservation. Includes a links page for children.
Species Survival Network CITES Conference
http://www.defenders.org/cites

Information on CITES conferences, including appendixes of endangered species.
World Rainforest Movement
http://www.wrm.org.uy/
Includes information on rainforests by country and by subject.
WWF–UK
http://www.wwf.org.uk/
In addition to its main website in the UK, the environmental organization has a number of sites devoted to different campaigns.
http://www.panda.org/
The international site for WWF.
http://www.panda.org/forest4life
The forests for life campaign.
Visit learn.co.uk for more resources

CD-ROM
Rainforest (Interfact) by Lucy Baker and Jason Page (Two-Can, 1998)

ADDRESSES OF ORGANIZATIONS
Friends of the Earth, 26-28 Underwood Street, London N1 7JQ Tel: 020 7490 1555
Web: http://www.foe.co.uk/
Greenpeace, Canonbury Villas, London N1 2PN
Tel: 020 7865 8100
Web: http://www.greenpeace.org.uk/
Oxfam, Oxfam House, Banbury Road, Oxford, OX2 7DZ Tel: 01865 312610
Web: http://www.oxfam.org.uk/
Survival International, 6 Charterhouse Buildings, London EC1M 7ET Tel: 0207 687 8700
Web: http://www.survival-international.org/
WWF–UK, Panda House, Weyside Park, Godalming, Surrey GU7 1XR
Tel: 01483 426444
Web: http://www.wwf.org.uk/

INDEX

Picture acknowledgements:
All photographs are by Edward Parker with the exception of the following: FLPA 7; OSF 13 bottom (Phil Devries), 27 bottom (J.A.L. Cooke), 29 top (J.A.L. Cooke), 31 top (Michael Fogden), 33 (Harold Taylor), 34 (Alistair Shay).